KT-116-064

A Rubber Tyre

Sarah Ridley

FRANKLIN WATTS

LONDON · SYDNEY

First published in 2005 by
Franklin Watts
96 Leonard Street
London
EC2A 4XD

Franklin Watts Australia
Level 17/207 Kent Street
Sydney NSW 2000

© Franklin Watts 2005

ISBN: 0 7496 6296 4
Dewey classification number: 678'.32

Series editor: Sarah Peutrill
Art director: Jonathan Hair
Design: Jemima Lumley

Printed in Malaysia

Photo credits: Richard Anthony/Holt Studios: 30b. Nigel Cattlin/Holt Studios: 6bl. Courtesy of John Deere: 25cl. Digital Vision: 12bl, 12tr. Mary Evans PL: 9b. Courtesy of Goodyear Dunlop: 20, 22, 27bl, 27tr. Hulton Deutsch/Corbis: 13b. Philippa Lewis/Corbis: 15b. Tom & Dee McCarthy/Corbis: 31. Michael Mathers/Still Pictures: 30t. Maximilian Stock Ltd/Science Photo Library: 15t, 16b, 24t, 27cr. Courtesy of Michelin: front cover tl, cl,c, cr, b & back cover. 1, 3, 4t, 4b, 5, 6tr, 11b, 14, 16t, 17t, 18, 21c, 25tr, 26tl, 26cl, 27tl, 27cla, 27clb. Shehzad Noorani/Still Pictures: 7, 8, 9t, 26bl, 26tr. Charles E. Rotkin/Corbis: 13t, 26br. Sipa Press/Rex Features: 23. Eric Smith. Art Directors/Trip: 11t. Inga Spence/Holt Studios: 10, 26cr.Topham: 17b, 19t. Courtesy of Volkswagon Group: 24b, 27br. Watts: 19b, 28, 29. Larry Williams/Corbis: 21b. Every attempt has been made to clear copyright. Should there be any inadvertent omission please apply to the publisher for rectification. With special thanks to Michelin and Goodyear Dunlop for their help with this book.

Contents

A car tyre is made of rubber.

A tyre's story starts with a rubber tree, which produces sap containing natural rubber, called latex. The rubber latex is mixed with synthetic rubber to make the tyre. After many stages in the factory, the tyre is fitted onto a car.

➤ Tyres help to make your car journey comfortable by smoothing out the bumps and gripping the road.

Rubber trees grow best in hot, wet climates. Around 85 per cent of rubber trees are grown on small family-owned plantations. The rest grow on large plantations - huge areas planted with trees.

◄ Tree sap carries food to all parts of the tree. The sap of the rubber tree, called latex, can be collected in cups.

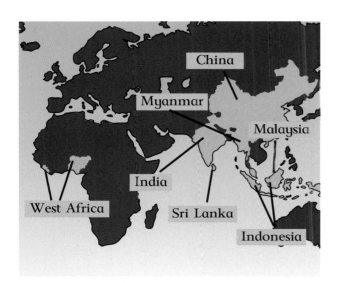

▲ The main countries that produce rubber today are marked in green.

Why rubber?

Natural rubber, or latex, has amazing properties. The main one is its elasticity - it can bend or stretch but will bounce back to its original shape. It is this elasticity that makes it suitable for tyres because when they go over bumps they give way, and then return to their shape. This helps passengers have a smooth ride. It also makes rubber perfect for bouncy balls!

New rubber trees are grown from seeds planted in pots and cared for in greenhouses.

▲ Scientists studied several types of rubber tree and found that these seedlings, *hevea brasiliensis,* produce the best rubber.

When the seedlings are strong, the workers plant them in nursery beds outside, and finally into rows.

Rubber trees are left to grow for six or seven years.

Now the rubber trees can be tapped for rubber latex. Each tapper owns or looks after certain trees on a plantation.

Early each morning the tapper cuts a strip of bark half way round each tree trunk, just below any previous cuts. The latex starts to flow, like blood out of a wound, into a collecting cup.

➤ A tapper on a rubber plantation slices away the bark to tap the tree.

◄ The latex flows from this recently tapped tree.

Later in the day, each tapper goes back to the same trees to collect the day's latex.

He or she empties the cups into a bucket and carries the bucket back to the village. After a few hours the trees heal their cuts and the latex stops flowing. The tapper will return to these trees two or three days later to tap them again.

▲ Tapper, Ma Than Than Htay (see next page), strains the day's latex.

In the past

In the 19th century, Britain controlled a vast area of the world through its empire. The British government set up botanical gardens in parts of the Empire, such as Sri Lanka, India and Singapore. In these gardens, people experimented with rubber plants, which had previously only grown in South America.

The rubber man

Henry Ridley, or 'Rubber' Ridley, was the director of the Botanical Gardens in Singapore from 1888 to 1911. From 22 rubber tree seedlings received by the gardens, he collected seeds to grow new plants for people interested in growing rubber trees in Malaysia. He also developed much better ways of tapping rubber trees. His work helped to establish a successful rubber industry in Asia.

The rubber processing begins.

▲ Ma Than Than Htay pours the creamy latex into shallow containers.

Now all the collected rubber latex is put together. Some plantations employ workers, some are run as cooperatives and others are run by families. Ma Than Than Htay lives in Myanmar in South-East Asia, and owns 1,200 rubber trees. With her family she taps latex and makes it into rubber sheets.

First she pours the creamy latex into shallow containers. Then she adds acid and leaves it to stand. The acid makes the small lumps that float in the liquid latex clump together. A thin layer of latex forms on the surface.

The layer of latex is lifted off and fed through rollers to squeeze out the water.

◄ Ma Than Than Htay's sons help her to put the latex sheets through rollers.

In the past

Until about 200 years ago, the South American Indians of the rainforest were the only people to tap rubber trees. They made rubber capes, shoes, torches and balls. To make rubber, they poured the liquid latex onto a small ball of rubber attached to a stick. The stick was held over a smoky, oily fire. The heat made the rubber in the latex stick to the ball of rubber. Gradually, the ball built up to a good size. Then the rubber worker started all over again.

A 19th-century drawing showing how South American Indians made rubber.

The rubber tappers hang out the sheets of latex to dry.

After the sheets have dried in the air, they are moved to smoke houses where the heat from fires dries them even more.

Each sheet is held up to the light to check the quality. The sheets with the least dirt in them are worth the most money. They are sorted by quality and packed into bales.

▲ Sheets of latex hang out to dry, like washing on a line.

Other latex is processed in factories. It goes through exactly the same stages, but on a larger scale. However, some latex goes through a different process. Castor oil is dribbled onto the sheets, which makes them break up into crumbs. These are dried and put in bags to be sold.

▲ In processing factories, everything happens on a bigger scale.

Now the latex is shipped to tyre factories. Tyre factories use 70 per cent of all the latex processed each year.

In the past

The first air-filled car tyre was invented by the Michelin brothers in 1895. Before this, many other people worked on tyre design, mostly for bicycles. In 1888, John Boyd Dunlop had the idea of trapping air inside a rubber tyre after watching his son struggling to ride a bicycle with solid rubber tyres.

The Michelin brothers amazed people in 1895 when they showed off their new air-filled tyres on a car called *Eclair*.

Synthetic rubber is made.

Just over half the rubber used to make tyres is synthetic. Synthetic rubber is made from oil and gas, rather than from tree sap. Oil is found under the sea or in the ground.

➤ Oil is removed from under the sea using a huge oil rig.

▲ At an oil refinery, oil is heated in tall towers.

The oil is taken to oil refineries. Here it is separated into different parts. Petrol, diesel and paraffin are taken away, leaving behind the parts of the oil that can be made into synthetic rubber. These are taken to the factories making synthetic rubber.

▲ This synthetic rubber factory stretches into the distance in Texas, USA.

Synthetic rubber factories treat the oil substances with chemicals, heat them to the right temperature and mix them with natural gas. The result is a substance that is stretchy and tough and very like natural rubber.

In the past

Scientists investigating natural rubber in the early 20th century found that they could make something similar from oil products. By World War II (1939-45), Germany, Russia, the USA and Britain were making large amounts of synthetic rubber. This helped them make enough tyres for all the war vehicles they needed at a time when it was difficult to obtain natural rubber from the other side of the world.

These huge tyres are causing trouble for two women war workers in 1943.

The rubber arrives at the tyre factory.

◄ Some of the many ingredients that make up a modern tyre, including oil, carbon black, rubber, steel wire and silica.

The synthetic rubber and latex make up about half of the ingredients needed to make a tyre. In all, around 200 different materials are used.

The first step is to mix the two sorts of rubber with oil, carbon black, silica, sulphur and various chemicals. The ingredients are weighed and added to a huge mixer.

In the mixer the ingredients warm up and gradually turn into a smooth, thick liquid.

▲ Scientists have worked out how much of each material is needed to make a good tyre.

Researchers work out which ingredients in the car tyre will make it perform the best. They use machines and computers to investigate how tyre materials stand up to use. These can put a computer-created tyre through its paces, instead of always using a real tyre.

Why add to rubber?

Rubber is naturally hard-wearing and tough. However, the other substances scientists have added to tyres make the rubber last longer and resist wear and tear.

Early tyres usually needed to be replaced after the car had been driven for 750-1,500 kilometres. Modern tyres can last for over 50,000 kilometres before wearing out.

COUPE des VOITURETTES 1907   NAUDIN sur SIZAIRE et NAUDIN

Like other tyre companies, Michelin developed close links with the sport of car racing, which showed off its tyres. This picture of a 1907 race in France is displayed at the company's original UK headquarters in London.

The rubber mixture is left to settle.

Some final ingredients are added and the whole mixture is pushed through a milling machine, between rollers. It comes out the other side as sheets of flat black rubber. These sheets are used to make the different parts of the tyre.

▲ The sticky rubber mixture is pushed through the milling machine.

▲ At every stage, the rubber is checked to ensure high quality.

Each part of the tyre is made separately. Here are the different parts.

The tread band runs in a ring around the tyre. The tread pattern helps the tyre to grip the road.

The body of the tyre is made up of a special fabric, which is made of layers of rubber material strengthened with synthetic or fabric cord.

The tyre beads are steel wire, pulled up tight around each edge of the tyre. They clamp the tyre onto the wheel rim.

At the centre of the tyre is a layer of airtight rubber.

The side walls are made from tough, flexible rubber to protect the side of the tyre.

In the past

The Michelin man is one of the world's best-known images. He was created in 1898 when André Michelin noticed that a pile of tyres could be made to look like a man by adding a head, arms and legs. The Michelin man was given a big stomach because he had eaten all the sharp objects that lay on roads at that time - horseshoes, nails, sharp rocks - showing that Michelin tyres were tough and would not puncture easily.

Le pneu Michelin boit l'obstacle means, 'The Michelin tyre drinks obstacles'.

Machines produce the different parts of the tyre.

In the factory the rubber is poured into moulds and squeezed through machines to produce shaped pieces.

The main part of the tyre (see page 17), or the carcass, is made using rubber and cord fabric. This is created by sandwiching metal or synthetic cords between sheets of rubber. Layers of this special fabric build up the strength and thickness of the tyre.

▲ Cords are lined up on a machine before being sandwiched in rubber to make the fabric for the main part of the tyre.

In the past

In the early 20th century, it was more difficult to find good tyres than good engines. Journeys were often delayed by punctures or blow-outs (burst tyres). Many motorists brought a mechanic along with them, mostly just to change the tyres!

The owners of this car look on while their mechanic mends their tyre at the roadside.

Why rubber?

Rubber is useful for tyres because it is waterproof and does not soak up water lying on the road. It is often used to make products that need to be waterproof. Water runs off rubber gloves, protecting the hands inside from the soapy water. Cloth can be coated with a thin layer of rubber (as left) to make it waterproof.

The tyre pieces are put together.

Each piece is placed in order on a metal drum. The workers start with the airtight inner rubber, then they lay the rubber fabric on top of that. Each time another layer is added, air is pushed out.

Next the tyre beads (see page 17) are placed on each outside edge. Then various shaped strips of rubber and the side walls are put in their correct position. Finally, the belt rubber and the flat tread band complete the tyre.

The worker builds up the tyre layers on a metal drum, starting with the airtight rubber at the centre.

At first the tread band is smooth, but later it will be imprinted with a pattern. The most important job of a tyre is to grip the road so that the driver can steer and keep control of the car. The tread helps the tyre to do this.

▼ Different tread patterns are used, depending on the weather and the roads the car will be driven on.

Why rubber?

When rubber warms up it naturally grips a surface, which is another reason to use rubber in tyres. Around 100 years ago, people noticed that rubber tyres with a tread pattern gripped the road even better. Tyre design and development has run alongside car design. As cars have become bigger and able to go faster, tyres have needed to change as well.

▼ In dry weather, racing car drivers use almost smooth tyres. At high speeds, the rubber in the tyres becomes hot and sticky, which helps the car to grip the track.

The tyre is heated in a mould.

While the tyre is in the mould, very hot water and steam heat the tyre materials, making them join together. The outside of the tyre pushes against the walls of the mould to imprint the tread design. This process is called curing and lasts for about 10 minutes at a temperature of around 150°C.

▲ The smooth tyre (bottom left) is about to go through the curing process. The top part of the moulding machine will come down to join the bottom part.

In the past

In countries like the USA where the weather ranges from very cold to hot, the early rubber macintoshes and other products turned sticky in hot weather and stiff in cold. This put people off buying rubber products. Then in 1841-42 Charles Goodyear discovered that if he added sulphur to natural rubber and then heated it, this made the rubber fix in the same state, regardless of the weather. He called the process vulcanisation.

During the curing process, the rubber is vulcanised. Because of the heat, the sulphur in the tyre makes the rubber fix in its final tyre shape. Before people discovered vulcanisation, finished rubber products continued to change shape in heat or cold.

▼ The tyres are released from the mould and move along a conveyor belt to be checked.

The last stage is to check the quality of the tyre.

The workers check each tyre as it comes out of the mould. This is the end of a long line of testing and checking.

► Scientists use computers and other machines to test car tyres at every stage.

At last, the tyres are ready to be fitted to the vehicle!

MBS 03·50

◄ Cars are just one type of vehicle that tyres are used on.

Today, tyres are made for all sorts of vehicles, from bicycles to space buggies, racing cars to monster trucks and tractors.

Each type of tyre uses slightly different materials and designs.

▲ Off-road cars have a deep tread pattern to grip in muddy conditions.

◄ Look at the size of these tyres! Huge tyres spread the tractor's weight and stop it sinking into soft ground.

How a rubber tyre is made

1. Rubber trees grow from seedlings. They take about six years to grow tall and strong.

4. The layers of rubber latex are put through rollers.

2. Tappers slice bark from rubber trees to collect the rubber latex.

5. The sheets of rubber latex hang out to dry.

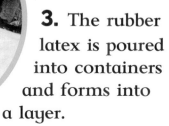

3. The rubber latex is poured into containers and forms into a layer.

6. Synthetic rubber is made in a factory, using oil substances.

7. The two sorts of rubber and around 200 other ingredients are mixed in the tyre factory.

11. The tyre is heated, or cured, in a mould.

8. The mixture goes through a milling machine to produce sheets of rubber.

12. The tyre is tested.

9. Machines make all the different parts of the tyre, coating cords with rubber.

10. The different parts of the tyre are put together on a drum.

13. The tyre rolls off the conveyor belt, leaves the factory, and is fitted to a car.

Rubber and its many uses

Rubber is a very useful material. It is stretchy, tough, waterproof, grips well and can be moulded into many shapes. It is used in many places around our homes and in our world.

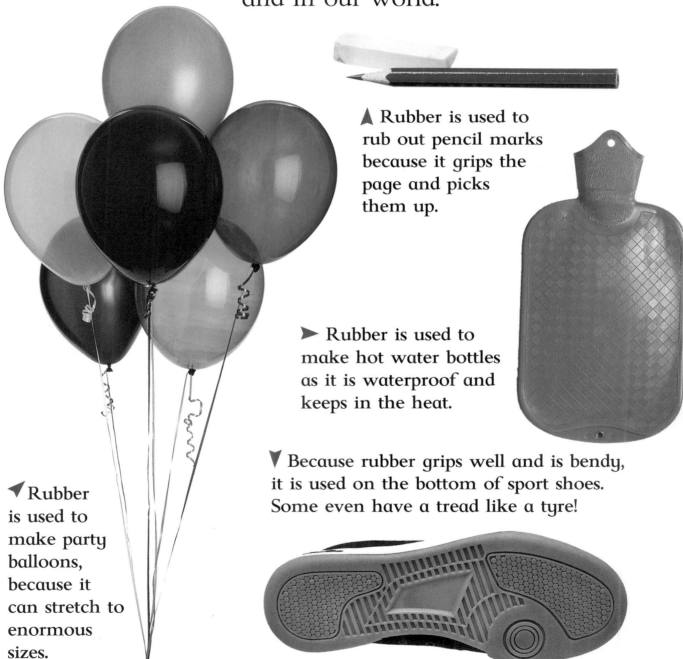

▲ Rubber is used to rub out pencil marks because it grips the page and picks them up.

► Rubber is used to make hot water bottles as it is waterproof and keeps in the heat.

▼ Because rubber grips well and is bendy, it is used on the bottom of sport shoes. Some even have a tread like a tyre!

◄ Rubber is used to make party balloons, because it can stretch to enormous sizes.

▼ Rubber is waterproof so it is used to make coats, boots and wetsuits.

◀ Because rubber does not let electricity flow through it, it is sometimes used to coat electric wires and make them safe.

▼ Rubber is used to create a seal on something - on a washing machine or round your swimming goggles.

▼ Rubber bands are very useful to keep things together.

How many other uses can you think of for rubber?

Tyres and the environment

Tyres wear out and create a problem as they don't rot away. Millions of tyres are thrown away every year, leaving tyre dumps around the world. There are various ways to tackle this.

▲ A tyre dump in the USA.

Research by tyre companies

Scientists employed by tyre companies experiment with different tyre materials and designs to see which last the longest time, and will help the car to use less fuel. Some tyres can be given a new tread if the rest of the tyre isn't too worn out. Truck tyres can sometimes be retreaded twice before becoming useless. Finally, tyre companies work with road-builders to design tyres that will produce the least noise, as road noise can seriously disturb people who live near busy roads.

▼ If a tyre is not too worn out, the tread can be replaced.

Drivers' responsibility

If tyres are kept with the correct amount of air in them (called air pressure), the tyres will last longer before they need replacing. Drivers should check this every week.

Re-using tyres

Used tyres can be shredded and burnt to provide energy for power stations. The smoke released when rubber burns is full of pollution so this has to be done carefully.

Some tyres are broken down into powder and used to make other rubber items. Some is mixed up with road surface materials to make roads. Some old tyres are used to edge docks to protect boats.

▲ Used rubber tyres are sometimes made into swings.

Word bank

Carbon black A form of carbon.

Climate The weather that usually occurs in an area.

Cooperative A group of people working together.

Drum A cylinder.

Elasticity The ability to be stretched and bent, and yet return to the original shape.

Empire A group of countries and people ruled by one powerful country.

Latex The milky juice of some plants that contains natural rubber.

Mechanic Someone skilled in mending and caring for cars.

Mould A container that gives shape to rubber and other materials.

To process To change a material by carrying out several actions on it.

Puncture A hole in a tyre that lets the air out.

Sap The liquid that flows around a plant, carrying food to all its parts.

Silica A form of sand.

Substance A type of material.

Sulphur A yellow element.

Synthetic A material made in a factory using chemicals.

Index